Bugs

Written by Emily Bone

Illustrated by Cinzia Battistel

Designed by Zoe Wray

Bugs consultant: Zoë Simmons
Reading consultant: Alison Kelly

There are all kinds of different bugs.

Some bugs can jump up high.

Grasshoppers

Other bugs have lots of legs.

Caterpillar

Centipede

Butterflies

Lots of bugs have wings.
They fly around.

Beetles

Some bugs don't have
any legs or wings.

Worm

Some bugs catch other bugs to eat.

A spider builds a web from sticky silk.

Golden orb weaver spider

Moth

A moth gets stuck in the web. The spider eats it.

Trapdoor spiders hide in burrows.

Trapdoor
spider

The spider spots a bug.

It jumps out of its burrow and
grabs the bug.

Bees and butterflies feed on flowers.

There is a sweet juice inside flowers called nectar.

6

They suck out
nectar with their
long tongues.

Some bugs build nests.

Wood ants make
big nests from twigs
and grass.

The ants carry the
pieces one at a time.

They dig long tunnels
under the ground too.

Young ants grow up in the tunnels.

Bees make nests too.

Honey bees
make nests
from wax.

Honey bee

The nests have lots of
little holes called cells.

10

A queen bee lays
eggs in the cells.

Young bees hatch out.

Worker bees feed
them with honey.

Queen bee

Some bugs look like other things.

A giant leaf insect
looks like a leaf.

Stick insects look
like twigs on trees.

Orchid mantises look like orchid flowers.

Dead leaf butterflies hide in brown leaves.

Some bugs are very big.

The atlas moth is the biggest flying bug.

This is the size it is in real life.

14

Atlas moth
caterpillar

15

Some bugs sting or bite.

Scorpion

Stinging tail

Cricket

Scorpions can sting to catch food.

Some caterpillars have stinging spines.
This stops them from being eaten.

Stag beetles
have big jaws.

They use their
jaws to fight
other beetles.

17

Slugs and snails don't have any legs.

Slug →

Their slimy
bodies help them
to slide along.

Snail →

Slime
trail

Snails have shells.

They can hide
their bodies
inside their shells.

Snails and slugs eat
the leaves of plants.

Bugs have babies. They look after them in different ways.

Wolf spiders carry their babies on their backs.

Shield bugs guard their babies under their bodies.

Leaf beetles lay eggs on leaves. The babies hatch out and eat the leaves.

Ants carry their babies
when they move nests.

A butterfly lays eggs on a plant.

Egg

A caterpillar hatches
from an egg.

It eats the plant.

It grows bigger
and bigger.

Its skin turns into
a hard case.

Its body changes
inside the case.
It becomes a butterfly.

Some bugs live in water.

Pond skaters balance
on the surface of water.

Great diving beetles
dive underwater to
catch food.

Stickleback fish

Water spiders live in webs under the water.

The web has air inside.
The spider breathes the air.

Shrimp

It comes out to catch food.

Other bugs grow up underwater.

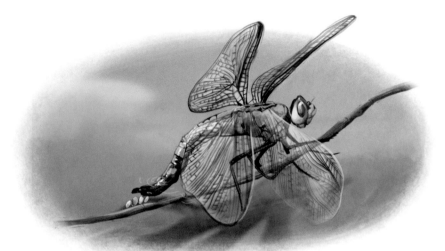

A dragonfly lays its eggs on a plant.

Young dragonflies hatch out. They are
called nymphs. They live underwater.

A nymph crawls out of the water.

It breaks out
of its skin...

...and becomes a dragonfly.

It flies away
to find food.

Old skin

Lots of bugs come out at night.

Some moths come out
to find partners.

Io moths

Luna
moth

Fireflies have
bodies that glow
in the dark.

Chirp
chirp!

Cicadas make a loud
chirping noise.

Most bugs can't live when it gets cold. Some find ways to stay warm.

Monarch butterflies fly to a place that has warmer weather.

Snails crawl under stones.
This keeps them warm.

Young
chafer
beetle

Young beetles live in the
warm ground.

In the spring, most bugs
come out again.

An adult chafer beetle
lives for just two weeks.

Digital retouching by John Russell